GREAT APES

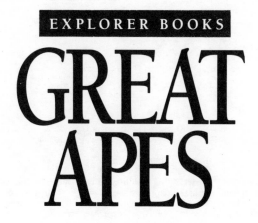

EXPLORER BOOKS

GREAT APES

by
Cathy East Dubowski

Published by The Trumpet Club
666 Fifth Avenue, New York, New York 10103

Copyright © 1991 Parachute Press, Inc.

ISBN: 0-440-84482-7

Printed in the United States of America
March 1991

10 9 8 7 6 5 4 3 2 1
CW

PHOTOGRAPH CREDITS

p. 29: top, © Miriam Austerman/Animals Animals; *bottom,* © Stewart D. Halperin/
Animals Animals. *p. 30:* © Tom McHugh, 1979/Photo Researchers, Inc. *p. 31:* ©
Gerry Ellis/Ellis Wildlife Collection. *p. 32: top,* UPI/Bettmann Newsphotos; *bottom,*
UPI/Bettmann. *p. 33:* Barry Shlachter/Gamma Liaison. *p. 34: top,* The Bettmann
Archive; *bottom,* © Russ Kinne 1989/Comstock. *p. 35: top,* © Tom McHugh, 1979/
Photo Researchers, Inc.; *bottom,* © George Holton/Photo Researchers, Inc. *p. 36:* © Joe
McDonald/Animals Animals.

Cover: © Jim Tuten 1986/Animals Animals

To my siblings—Cheryl, John, and Christel,
and with special thanks to my editor, Ruth Koeppel

Contents

Introduction

Deep in the African rain forest, a slender, young English woman made her way slowly and quietly through the jungle. She was all alone. Vine-covered trees towered above her. Insects buzzed in the air, and exotic birds entertained her with their songs. Lizards and other unseen creatures rustled through the lush undergrowth.

Jane Goodall had been wandering patiently through the forest on this mountain slope since 5:30 A.M. She was hunting. But she was not hunting with a gun. She carried only a notebook and pencil, plus a kettle and a tin mug for making coffee. Her aim was not to capture or kill her prey. She wanted only to watch and learn.

Would she be lucky today? Would she come face to face with a chimpanzee?

Jane was staying at the Gombe Stream Reserve in an African country called Tanzania. Her mission: to study chimpanzees in their natural habitat—far from the cages and curious crowds of zoos.

At first she caught only rare glimpses of the apes, or heard their chattering through the trees. Gradually some of the chimps lost their fear of her. Jane was able to move closer and closer to watch them. Some even scampered into her camp to feast on the ripe fruit she left out for them!

Jane was beginning to learn firsthand what life was really like for chimpanzees in the wild. But the more she learned, the more she wanted to know. So she spent every day from dawn till dusk exploring the forests.

Then one day Jane saw something amazing. She was walking through the woods. Suddenly she stopped. Right in front of her, a chimpanzee was hunched over an earth-packed termite mound. Jane smiled. It was a chimp she had seen many times before. She had named him David Greybeard, because of the thick grey hairs that covered his chin.

Jane waited quietly, eager to see what he might do.

David Greybeard picked a blade of grass and stuck it in the hole of the termite mound. When he pulled it out, it was covered with termites. He quickly gobbled up every one of the juicy black insects. After a few more mouthfuls, though, the blade of grass bent in half. Now it was useless.

2

David found a twig and examined it. Then he picked off all the leaves. Finally satisfied, he fished in the hole with the twig and brought up another delicious serving of termites.

Jane was thrilled! She had seen an *animal* use a tool.

Even more exciting, she had seen something no one had ever seen before.

She had watched an animal *make* a tool.

You may think this sounds simple. You use tools every day: a knife, fork, and spoon to eat. A pair of scissors to cut out paper dolls. A hammer and saw to build a doghouse.

But until Jane saw David Greybeard use his "termite tool," scientists believed that only humans had the intelligence to make tools. David Greybeard proved them wrong.

This single observation changed forever the way many people look at animals. And it added to many scientists' growing belief in the intelligence of chimpanzees and other apes.

For centuries people have been fascinated by apes. Chimpanzees were brought to Europe by explorers. They were dressed up like people and taught to do entertaining tricks at court! Gorillas were portrayed as terrifying, bloodthirsty monsters in movies like *King Kong*. Orangutans delighted zoo visitors with their red hair and their humorous expressions.

But for the past 30 years some scientists have been seriously challenging old ideas and myths about apes. They've studied apes in the laboratory and in the wild. And they've asked some startling questions.

Do apes think? Do they feel emotions like love and hate? Can they communicate with people? Is it only by chance that they look and act like humans? What can we learn from these animals?

But we may have waited too long to care about these fascinating creatures. Over the past 50 years all the great apes—gorillas, chimpanzees, and orangutans—have begun to disappear from the Earth. And humans are responsible. People hunted and killed them. People destroyed their forest homes to harvest timber, to plant new fields, or to build villages and roads.

So now scientists have the most important question of all to ask about apes:

Will there be any left when *you* grow up?

In this book you'll find out what the great apes are *really* like and why scientists are so excited about them. And you'll find out what you can do to help save their lives in the wild.

1

Meet the Great Apes

Why do humans find apes so interesting?

For many people it's because the great apes—chimpanzees, gorillas, and orangutans—seem to be like humans in so many ways. In the animal kingdom, apes are mankind's closest living relative.

Humans and the great apes both belong to a group of animals called *mammals*—warm-blooded, hairy creatures that give birth to live babies.

Apes have large brains that are physically similar to humans'. They have shown an ability to think, communicate, and learn.

If you shook hands with an orangutan, you'd see and feel how much ape hands are like your own hands. Unlike dogs, horses, or bears, apes have movable fingers and toes. Even more important, apes, like humans, have opposable thumbs—thumbs that can work independently of the other fingers. So apes can grasp things, carry things, climb easily, and even hold hands.

Their feet work almost as well as their hands. Their big toes are like thumbs, which help them grab onto branches when they climb. Human feet are not quite so "handy." But if you try to pick up a marble or a pencil with your toes, you'll see that you too have some of this ability.

Examine the tips of your fingers. The swirling patterns in the skin are called fingerprints. Your fingerprints are different from anybody else's in the world. Police officers can often identify crooks by their fingerprints. Apes have their very own fingerprints, too. Gorillas even have their very own one-of-a-kind noseprints!

Apes have upright skeletons, similar to those of humans, which allow them to walk on two legs for short distances. And when they do walk on all fours like dogs or horses, they walk on the knuckles of their hands.

Who would you guess has more hair? A human or an ape? If you guessed an ape, you're wrong. Humans have the same number of hairs on their bodies as apes do. Look closely at your arms and face, hands and stomach. You'll see many tiny fine hairs. Human hairs don't grow long into a thick coat like an ape's.

What fascinates scientists even more than these external similarities is that humans and apes are alike in some ways on the inside. For example, under a microscope, ape blood and human blood are almost identical.

Don't sneeze on an ape—it might catch your cold. Apes can become infected with almost every illness that humans can, from the common cold to chicken pox. *Pediatricians*—doctors who treat children—often treat baby gorillas in zoos.

The similarities between apes and humans are almost eerie. What does it all mean?

No one knows for sure. In the early 1900's, a scientist named Charles Darwin developed the study of *evolution*. Darwin explained how all living mammals are related, some more closely than others. He studied how traits are passed down from parents to children.

Today most scientists believe that humans and apes evolved from a common ancestor called *proconsul* that lived some 15 to 20 million years ago. Over thousands of years, both cave people and apes *evolved* from this common ancestor. Apes are being studied both in the laboratory and in the wild to see if they hold clues to human existence.

2

Where To Find an Ape

You may have seen chimpanzees, gorillas, and orangutans in a zoo. But where would you go to find apes in the wild?

Scientists believe that centuries ago apes may have lived in many areas of the world. A legendary apelike creature called the Yeti supposedly roams the snowy mountains of the Himalayas. In 1951, an English explorer named Eric Shipton took photographs of huge footprints in the snow that he claimed were made by this "abominable snowman." In 1967, near Bluff Creek, California, Roger Patterson videotaped what he thought to be Bigfoot, another legendary apelike creature.

Some *zoologists*—scientists who study animals —are fascinated by the possibility that these creatures exist. Others say these stories are ridiculous. No one knows for sure.

But the great apes you'll learn about in this book live in central Africa along the equator and in Southeast Asia. The jungles and rain forests in

8

these areas provide apes with the food and protected environment they need to survive.

Chimpanzees

Fifty years ago millions of chimpanzees roamed the forests of more than twenty-five African countries in western and central Africa along the equator. Today they are found in far fewer countries and in more scattered groups. Many chimps live in dense tropical rain forests or jungles. Others live in drier forests along the rivers or in open savannas. Scientists estimate that there are only 145,000 to 200,000 chimps still living in the wild.

The scientific name for the chimpanzee is *Pan troglodytes*. Chimps are the most intelligent of all the apes. They have good memories, they reason well, and they're very quick to learn.

Chimps can be found in many zoos and are often seen on television shows and commercials. Their skin color ranges from light to dark. But most are covered with thick black hair, with little or no hair on their faces or on the palms of their hands and feet. But just like some humans, they often grow bald as they grow older! Chimps have a long life span, too—they can live to be 50 or 60 years old.

Chimpanzees are the smallest of the great apes. If you could get one to stand up straight—and still!—long enough to be measured, you'd find him to be about the same height as a second grader. A male chimp will grow to be about 4 feet tall and weigh about 100 pounds with an arm spread of up to 9 feet. Even so, he'll be three times as strong as a man twice his size! A female chimp will grow almost as tall as a male.

Chimpanzees live in a community of about 60 to 80 members. But within that community, chimps often move around in smaller family groups.

A mother chimp and her children are almost always together. Young chimps travel with their mother until they are about 7 or 8 years old. Mother chimps are very loving and gentle with their babies. They hold them a lot and hug them often—and even tickle them sometimes! They stroke and comfort the babies when they are frightened. A baby travels by hanging onto its mother's chest fur. Older chimps ride on their mothers' backs.

Often grown male chimps like to travel through the forest in all-male groups. Other times they travel with a brother or close male friend or wander off by themselves.

Most of the time, however, chimps are very social animals. They have their own way of communicating—and use more than thirty different sounds. Sometimes they make what sounds like a *pant-hoot*. A chimp who sees danger will make a loud, terrifying *wraaaa* sound. A sad baby chimp might make a gentle *hoo* sound.

Chimps also use very dramatic body language. They gesture with their hands. They may bow or swagger or hold hands with each other. Their faces express anger, joy, and fear.

Chimps often groom each other. For hours they will run their fingers through each other's hair, picking out debris. This keeps their coats clean. But it is also a way chimpanzees show affection or try to calm down an excited or angry friend or family member.

Chimps usually travel on the ground on all fours, though sometimes they stand upright. But they are good climbers and like to spend time in the trees, too, especially when looking for food. Chimps usually eat fruit and other plants. But sometimes they hunt and will eat small animals, such as baby monkeys or baboons. At night they build nests in the trees. They sleep as high as 100 feet off the ground!

Chimps in Space

In the early days of the space program, scientists wanted to see if it was safe for humans to go into space. What would happen to people if they traveled at such high speeds in a state of weightlessness?

Scientists had already sent mice, rabbits, dogs, and monkeys into space. But they still had many questions. The body of a chimpanzee is similar to that of a human astronaut. Scientists could study the effects of space travel on a chimp's body and learn a great deal about how space travel would affect a person.

Twenty chimps were trained at Holloman Air Force Base in New Mexico. They had to learn how to sit still strapped in a chair for long periods of time and how to operate levers in response to different colored flashing lights. Then they were placed in space capsules and were put through tests that simulated real trips in space. Testing them was not easy. When they pulled the right lever, they were rewarded with food or something to drink. If they made a mistake, they got an electric shock. Each chimp was trained for over a thousand hours!

Some chimps didn't like to be strapped in. Others wouldn't do the work or didn't work hard enough.

At last scientists chose a chimp—a $3\frac{1}{2}$-year-old named Ham, who had scored the highest on all the tests. In January 1961, Ham was brought to Cape Canaveral and strapped into a Mercury Redstone space capsule. Scientists watched him through a TV camera as the countdown began: 10, 9, 8, 7 . . . blastoff! Ham shot into space at 5,000 miles an hour. He performed all his tests well and came back safe and sound. Ham's voyage convinced scientists that it was safe to send a person into space.

Four months later, on May 5, 1961, Alan Shepard became the first American to take off into space.

On November 29, 1961, a chimp named Enos orbited the Earth. He too came back safe and sound. On February 20, 1962, John Glenn became the first American to orbit the Earth. Chimps paved the way for the astronauts' success!

Gorillas

Gorillas can be found in the tropical forests and mountains of central Africa. The western lowland gorillas *(Gorilla gorilla gorilla)* live in the Congo River Basin. These gorillas are the ones most often found in zoos. The mountain gorillas *(Gorilla gorilla beringei)* live on the slopes of the Virunga volcanoes along the borders of Rwanda, Uganda, and Zaire. In the surrounding areas live the eastern lowland gorillas *(Gorilla gorilla graueri)*—only recently grouped separately from mountain gorillas. Scientists estimate that there are only about 3,000 to 5,000 lowland gorillas and 300 to 500 mountain gorillas living in Africa today.

When Western explorers and missionaries first saw gorillas in the mid-1800's, they brought back horror stories about these "evil monsters." African legends called gorillas "black devils" or the souls of the "uneasy dead." Some natives believed that if a person cut off the toes and fingers of a gorilla and cooked them, the magic potion would give him great powers.

Full-grown gorillas certainly can look frightening. A male can grow up to 6 feet tall with an arm spread of 9 feet and can weigh as much as 450 pounds. When he thinks his group is being threatened, he puts on a terrifying show. He roars and pretends to charge. He beats his chest and makes a loud drumming sound that can be heard up to a mile away. Angrily he rips plants from the ground and throws them at the enemy. Then he thumps the ground as if to say "So there!"

The gorilla that usually puts on this terrifying show is the leader of the group, called a male silverback because of the streak of silver grey hairs that appears on a male gorilla when he is about 10 years old. He is the protector of a group of 5 to 20 gorillas that live together as a family. Most are female gorillas, their babies, and other young gorillas. When the males are grown, they leave the group to lead their own gorilla "family."

Gorillas almost always have black skin covered with thick black hair. Yet in October 1966, Africans shot and killed a female lowland gorilla who was raiding a banana plantation. Huddled beside the dead ape was something no one had ever seen before: a white ape. The gorilla crouching beside its dead mother became known as Snowflake. He has pale skin, snow-white fur, and pinkish pale-blue eyes. Snowflake is an *albino*—he does not have *melanin*, pigment that gives animals and people the color in their hair and skin. Today Snowflake lives in Spain at the Barcelona Zoo. He has fathered two children—both regular black apes. But scientists are watching and waiting to see if one of those gorillas will one day have an albino child.

In the movie *King Kong*, the giant ape was a bloodthirsty monster who chomped people between his huge teeth. But in fact gorillas are 100 percent *vegetarians*—they do not eat any kind of meat. But it takes a lot of fruit, flowers, bamboo,

14

and leaves to fill up a 450-pound silverback! So gorilla families spend much of their day traveling through the rain forest looking for food. In the middle of the day they stop and rest. The adults doze. Gorillas in general are calmer and quieter than chimpanzees. But the high-spirited young gorillas wrestle, play games, and practice thumping their chests, imitating the old silverback.

Gorillas, like all apes, are good climbers. Perhaps because of their size, though, they spend most of their time on the ground. Each night gorillas stop wherever they are and make new nests of leaves and twigs in the forks of trees. But grown gorillas are heavy, so they build their nests only 10 feet or so above the ground.

Orangutans

Orangutans are the "redheads" of the ape family. Their long, shaggy reddish-orange hair and expressive faces have made them favorites at zoos. That's one reason that there are not many living in the wild anymore. Researchers estimate that there are no more than 30,000 living in the wild today.

Orangutans were once found in Asia. But today they live only in the swampy coastal forests of Indonesia, on the islands of Borneo and Sumatra. People have known about orangutans for centuries. But orangutans are very shy and hard to find, so we still don't know much about them.

Orangutans are so shy—and are such good

climbers—that they almost never come down out of the trees. At night they sleep in nests built high in the branches.

An orangutan's hair can range from reddish brown to orange, with skin that's grey or sandy-colored. A grown male weighs about the same as a grown human male—between 150 and 200 pounds. But the tallest they ever get is about 4½ feet. Orangutans are round, short, and bowlegged. Their arms are longer than their legs. So when they do come down to the ground, they're very awkward.

Orangutans have strong arms and are well built for climbing. Yet they almost always travel very slowly—as if they were tired. They test each branch carefully, and only let go with one hand at a time. They can use their feet as easily as their hands. Often they just hang in the trees and swing lazily from their arms and legs—like a living hammock!

Young orangutans love to play, just like the young of other apes. But they change as they grow older. Unlike gorillas and chimps, adult orangutans are loners. There is no brawling among adult males to decide who will be the next leader of a community group—because they do not live in groups. They live like hermits, wandering the forests alone, hidden away high up in the trees. When a male groans and roars, he is warning other males away from his space. The female travels with only her children.

With their large, dark eyes, orangutans have

perhaps the most expressive faces of all the apes. They often look as though they were making funny faces.

Adult male orangutans have large pouches of skin on their cheeks and hanging down under their chins. It makes them look like funny old men. In the Malay language, *orangutan* means "old man of the forest."

Beneath these large cheeks are air sacs that the orangutan uses to make sounds—deep roaring groans, sighs, even loud burping noises! Scientists aren't sure what these sounds mean, but they seem to be ways of communicating.

3

Talking Chimps

Have you ever wished you could talk to an animal? For centuries most people believed that animals could not think, feel, or reason. They believed that the ability to use language—to communicate with words—was something that set people apart from animals.

But some people began to question that idea. And we now know that some animals—especially apes—are able to learn some elements of human language.

Viki

In 1916 William H. Furness worked every day for six months trying to teach an orangutan how to talk. But the ape learned to say only two words: *papa* and *cup*. Furness claimed that his orangutan called out "Cup, cup" as a way of asking for water when she was dying of the flu.

In the 1940's two scientists named Keith and

Catherine Hayes tried to teach a baby chimp named Viki how to speak English. They raised Viki in their home, as if she were a human baby. She was playful, bright, and affectionate. She liked to play and loved to be tickled. But after years of daily training, Viki could say only four words: *mama, papa, up,* and *cup.* And Viki's "mama" and "papa" were just about the only people who could understand what she was saying.

Both Furness's orangutan and Viki seemed to be very bright. They could learn to do many things that humans can do. Viki even learned to sweep with a broom and change her own clothes. Why couldn't these apes learn to talk?

Many people saw these experiments as failures. Some scientists said that because apes could not speak, it was proof that they were not smart enough to think or learn language.

But in 1969 Dr. Philip Lieberman of the University of Connecticut discovered a physical reason why apes could not learn to speak. He studied the vocal tracts in chimpanzees' throats and found that they are very different from those of humans. Apes' vocal tracts are too narrow and inflexible to make most of the sounds that form human words. They also can't move their tongues the way humans do. And chimps don't use their lips while making sounds.

The fact is that even humans don't have to be able to speak to use language. Many people who are deaf and have never learned to speak communicate well with their hands. They shape their fingers into patterns that stand for letters and words. They communicate by using American Sign Language.

Apes' hands are very much like human hands. And apes use facial expressions and gestures along with sounds. Could apes be taught to "speak" with sign language?

The Gardners Adopt Washoe

In the 1960's, animal traders stalking the African wilds killed a mother chimpanzee and captured her baby. This baby chimp, like many others, was sold to the U.S. Air Force for space program experiments.

But this chimp never made it into outer space. In June 1966, when she was about a year old, the chimp went to live with psychologists Allen and Beatrix Gardner of the University of Nevada at Reno. They named the chimp Washoe, after the county where the university is located. They raised her at their home, surrounded by lots of love—and lots of toys!

The Gardners had seen films of the chimp Viki trying to talk. They felt sure that her problems were physical—that her body parts were not really capable of making the sounds needed to speak. But they believed her facial expressions and gestures showed that she was trying to communicate.

Now the Gardners wanted to try to teach Washoe to talk. But instead of the spoken word, they taught her American Sign Language, or Ameslan (ASL). ASL is a complete language with its own grammatical system. It requires complex hand movements.

The Gardners tried to teach Washoe how to hold her hands to make words. What worked the best was a technique called *molding*. First they showed Washoe an object. Then they molded her hand into the right sign. Gradually she learned to make the sign herself.

Washoe loved to be tickled. When one of the Gardners stopped tickling her, she took his or her hands and put them back on her ribs! The Gardners decided to use this gesture in teaching signs. They noticed that she would often put her hands over the spot where she was being tickled— just as a ticklish human might. So the Gardners would tickle her, then stop. If Washoe put her hands together over her stomach, they would tickle her again. Washoe began to use the gesture to ask to be tickled. Gradually the Gardners changed the gesture until it looked like an Ameslan sign. Washoe began to put just her fingertips together in front of her. At last Washoe had learned her very first sign: the word for *more*. More tickling! She really understood the sign— she soon used it to ask for more pillow fights or more food.

After that, Washoe quickly learned more words: *sweet, toothbrush,* and *drink.* Next she was taught pronouns—words like *you* and *me.* Very soon she began to use two or three words together. Her first "sentences" were *Gimme sweet, Come open,* and *You tickle me.* When she looked in a mirror, she signed, *That me Washoe.* Washoe learned to make these word combinations at about the same age that human children do—between 18 and 24 months.

One might have expected Washoe to start out by learning signs for nouns—names of things, like *hat, ball,* or *banana.* But from the very beginning she used signs that expressed ideas or feelings. She signed, for example, *I hurt, funny, please,* and *I'm sorry.*

Washoe also showed that she understood the true meaning of the words she was learning. She would sign *dog* when she saw not only a real dog, but also a picture of a dog. She would use the word *baby* to mean a human baby or an animal baby.

The Gardners kept a careful diary of everything Washoe said. After three years with the Gardners, Washoe's vocabulary list included 85 signs. She regularly combined them to create "sentences." After four years she had learned 130 signs.

Washoe was *communicating* with humans. She was the first animal to use sign language to "talk" to people. She changed forever the belief that animals do not think or have feelings.

Washoe and the Fouts

When Washoe was five, her training was taken

over by Roger Fouts, a graduate student who had worked with the Gardners.

More than twenty years later Dr. Fouts and his wife, Debbi, continue to work with Washoe. She lives at the psychology department of Central Washington University in Ellensburg, Washington, with four other chimps: Dar, Tatu, Moja, and Loulis. Washoe has adopted Loulis as her son.

Washoe and the other chimps live in four room-size cages connected by walkways. They have lots of toys to play with. Toothbrushes are among their favorite toys, and they are very good about brushing their teeth. Moja likes to play with Velcro. They also like to play dress up and wear Halloween masks. They love to eat sweets—cookies, jelly beans, chewing gum—and aren't shy about asking for more in sign language.

Roger and Debbi and a staff of trained volunteers spend a great deal of time every day talking with the chimps. But they know it can be boring to practice the same words over and over again. They talk about fun things, like food, toys, and books. They ask a lot of questions, like *What?, Whose?,* and *What color?* Chimps learn more when school is fun!

Roger points out that Washoe has made up some of her own signs. One day Roger and Washoe saw a swan gliding on a lake. Washoe had never seen a swan before. In sign language Roger asked her, *What is it?* Washoe made up her own sign for *swan* by putting together two words that she already knew: *water* plus *bird* to make *water bird.*

Another time she called a sweet slice of juicy watermelon a *candy drink*. Once Moja put together two words to name a fizzling glass of Alka-Seltzer: *listen drink*.

When Washoe adopted baby Loulis, the Fouts decided to try a new experiment. They taught Loulis only seven signs: *who, what, where, which, want, name,* and *sign*. They were very careful not to use sign language with Washoe when Loulis was watching.

As the Fouts had hoped, Loulis soon began to use signs! He began to sign words like *hot* and *hurry*. Then one day the Fouts saw Loulis sign the word *hug*—to Washoe! Something very special had happened. Washoe had taught Loulis sign language. Loulis quickly learned more than fifty-five signs from Washoe and the other chimps.

The Fouts decided to videotape the chimps when they were alone. They found out that the chimps talked to themselves and to each other with sign language—even when there were no humans around!

The Fouts have dedicated their entire lives to raising, teaching, and studying Washoe, Loulis, Dar, Tatu, and Moja. Their research is helping humans understand language and has led to new ways of treating human children with mental disorders and learning disabilities.

The Fouts have also set up an organization called Friends of Washoe. They share their research about chimps learning sign language. They hope to save chimpanzees in the wild and to improve conditions for chimps living in zoos and laboratories.

Through Friends of Washoe, the Fouts are also raising money to build an indoor-outdoor habitat at Central Washington University that will give their chimps more freedom.

4

Koko the Gorilla

On July 4, 1971, the San Francisco Zoo had more than the birth of our country to celebrate. Jackie, one of their gorillas, gave birth to a baby girl. Gorillas do not mate well in captivity, so each new baby is very special. The zookeepers named her Hanabi-Ko, which means "fireworks child" in Japanese. But everyone has always called her Koko.

When Koko was three months old she grew very ill with an intestinal disease. The zookeepers thought she might die. She had to be taken away from her mother to be treated.

Koko and Penny

A group of volunteers took turns feeding and cuddling Koko. One of them was Francine "Penny" Patterson, a graduate student from Stanford University. Penny had once heard the

Gardners speak about their work with Washoe. She was fascinated. She began to think that she, too, would be interested in working with apes.

Penny began to spend more and more time at the zoo. She asked the director of the zoo for permission to work with Koko and teach her ASL. But he was afraid that Koko would become attached to Penny and after a few weeks she would leave. Then Penny told him she would be willing to make a commitment to work with Koko for four or five years. The director agreed to Penny's plan—and Project Koko began. It was the first time that anyone had tried to do this kind of research with a gorilla.

Koko was a quick learner, and she soon began to learn sign language. Within two months Koko had learned to sign sixteen word combinations, such as *more food*. In 1974 the project was moved to Stanford University, where Koko lived most of the time in a five-room trailer on campus. Penny bought Koko from the zoo and set up the Gorilla Foundation, a nonprofit organization to raise money to fund the project.

In April 1979 Penny graduated with her Ph.D. in developmental psychology, based on her work with Koko. Koko was almost 8 years old. Stanford University officials were beginning to worry that Koko might escape and hurt someone. So Penny had to find a new home for her gorilla. At last she found an old farm for sale in Woodside, California. She bought the farm and moved there to continue her research.

Gorilla Sign Language

Penny used molding to teach Koko signs, just as Roger and Debbi Fouts had with Washoe. But gorilla hands are not as flexible as chimpanzee hands. Koko had trouble making some of the ASL signs. So Penny made a few changes and nicknamed their version "Gorilla Sign Language" (GSL).

Penny and her assistants watch Koko closely and keep very detailed records of the signs she uses. Today Koko's "official" vocabulary list includes over 600 words. Penny claims that Koko probably knows at least 1,000. And she estimates that Koko uses about 100 different signs every day.

Koko doesn't know just the signs for things, like ball, gorilla, and toothbrush. Penny says that Koko knows also how to "talk" about feelings and thoughts. She knows signs for *bad, boring,* and *funny.*

Once Koko was supposed to be cleaning up her room. But when Penny turned her back, Koko tore up a sponge into tiny pieces. Penny pointed to the pieces of sponge on the floor and signed, *What is this?* Koko tucked her head down and put her hands over her ears—the sign for *trouble.*

Another time Koko saw a picture of a horse being yanked by the reins with the bit cutting into its mouth. Koko signed, *Horse sad.* When someone asked her why, Koko answered, *Teeth.*

Just as with Washoe, there are scientists who

Gorilla parents cuddle their newborn baby in the San Francisco Zoo. In the wild, the father would leave the mother and baby to fend for themselves.

A mother with her baby looks on as one chimp grooms another at the Gombe Stream Reserve in Tanzania.

An orangutan mother cares for her baby in Sabah, Borneo.

Jane Goodall mimics the behavior of chimps while studying them in their natural habitat.

Washoe uses sign language to tell Dr. Roger Fouts that she'd like some fruit.

In 1974, Penny Patterson brought 3-year-old Koko to Stanford University so she could continue teaching her Gorilla Sign Language.

Dian Fossey stands near the grave of Uncle Bert in the cemetery she built for wild mountain gorillas murdered by poachers.

Doctors unzip Ham's space suit after the chimp's famous trip into space in 1961. After traveling at 5,000 miles per hour, Ham was in great shape.

Chimps can live for 50 to 60 years. Like people, aging chimps may lose their hair.

Amazingly enough, chimps can invent tools. This one uses a crumpled leaf as a sponge to absorb water for drinking.

High up in the trees, a chimp uses a twig as a tool to clean his teeth.

A lowland gorilla from Zaire beats on his chest with his hands to show who's boss.

don't believe Koko is really using language. But Penny points out that when Koko meets new people, she immediately tries to talk to them and ask questions in sign language. And when Koko looks at picture books, she often makes signs—or "talks" to herself—about what she's "reading."

Koko and Michael

Today Koko lives in a group of trailers with a male gorilla named Michael, who has also learned sign language. Koko is 5 feet and 3/4 of an inch tall and weighs 250 pounds. Her favorite color is red, and her favorite foods are nuts, corn on the cob, and apples. She likes to play with dolls, read, draw, and chase Michael.

Michael, who is a couple of years younger than Koko, is 6 feet tall and weighs 425 pounds. He has told his teachers that his favorite color is yellow and his favorite food is peanut butter sandwiches. He likes to play with sounds and rhythms, look at pictures, and chase Koko.

Koko and Michael often act like jealous siblings. Michael gets mad if Koko gets too much attention from visitors. They love to wrestle and pick on each other, especially when they think no one is watching. They even call each other names when they get angry at each other! Once Koko used signs to call Michael a *toilet devil*. Michael came back with *stink bad squash gorilla lip*. (*Lip* is the sign Koko and Michael use to mean "woman.") One day a volunteer asked Michael,

Who ripped my jacket? Michael signed, *Koko.* Suspicious, the volunteer asked again, *Who ripped my jacket?* At last Michael admitted he did it.

Most of the time, however, the two gorillas seem to be the best of friends. Once Michael bit a male visitor who he thought was trying to hurt Koko. Sometimes he makes loud barking noises when he sees human males showing Koko too much affection. Once a volunteer asked Koko, *What do you say to Mike when you play?* Koko answered, *Mike Koko love.*

Koko's Cat

One year Koko got a present that made her famous.

Her birthday was coming up, and Penny asked her what she wanted for a present.

Cat, signed Koko. Penny was not surprised. After all, Koko's two favorite stories were *Puss in Boots* and *The Three Little Kittens.*

But Penny had trouble finding a toy cat that Koko wouldn't tear up easily. At last she found one in a catalog. It was a cement cat covered with vinyl and black velvet. But it didn't come till after Koko's birthday, so Penny saved it for a Christmas present.

At last Christmas morning arrived. Koko got lots of presents, including nuts and a doll. But when Koko opened the present Penny had been saving for her, she did something that really surprised Penny.

Koko signed, *That red.*

What did Koko mean? Have you ever heard the expression to "see red" when you're angry? When Koko got angry, she would often sign *red.*

She was angry about the cat! She began to run around the room and bang the walls.

At last Penny figured out what was wrong. Koko didn't want a toy cat—she wanted a real one!

One day a friend brought over three stray kittens. Koko picked a grey tabby without a tail. For several days the kitten was brought for a visit so Koko could get used to it. Koko would blow on the cat and cuddle it. When the kitten stuck out her claws, Koko signed, *Cat do scratch. Koko love.* Koko named it All Ball.

At first Penny would let Koko play with All Ball only when she was around. But she soon learned that Koko was gentle with her, even when the kitten bit Koko. Koko even carried All Ball on her back as if she were a baby gorilla.

Then one day All Ball got hit by a car. When Penny told Koko the news, Koko made long, sad hoots. A few days later she signed, *Sleep cat* and *Cry, sad, frown.*

After a while Penny gave Koko a new kitten. But Michael, who is much bigger than Koko, wanted it, so Koko let him have it. At last Penny found Koko a little grey cat. Koko named it Smoky.

Penny had promised the zoo director that she would spend four or five years with Koko. Instead, she has spent her entire career studying and teaching Koko and Michael.

Penny hopes one day to set up a gorilla preserve for Koko and Michael. Through the Gorilla Foundation she is raising funds to buy a large piece of land, perhaps in Hawaii. There the gorillas could live outdoors and have more freedom. In a more natural setting Michael and Koko might mate and have children. Perhaps they'll be the first apes to pass sign language on to the next generation!

5

In the Land of the Apes

Humans have learned a great deal from apes in zoos and laboratories. But these apes have been taken out of their natural habitat. Sometimes they become so comfortable around humans that they don't do things they would have learned naturally if they lived in the jungle. For example, mother apes in zoos who have not grown up around other females often don't know how to care for their own babies. They neglect them or hurt them, and zookeepers have to raise the babies separately.

Apes in captivity such as Washoe and Koko have learned many fascinating things, including sign language. This research is very important to our understanding of humans and animals. But it is only part of the story.

Naturalists who study apes in the wild try very hard not to affect the behavior of the animals they're watching. Instead of teaching apes human ways, these researchers try to blend in with the apes. They follow the wandering apes alone or in very small groups. They watch quietly and calmly, trying not to make sudden moves. They let the apes get used to them slowly. This way they can get a clear picture of what life is *really* like for apes in the wild.

George B. Schaller

It wasn't until 1959 that a scientist used careful scientific methods—and a great deal of patience— to discover the true nature of apes.

George B. Schaller was an *ethologist*—a scientist who studies animal behavior under natural conditions. He and his wife, Kay, lived in a hut in the Albert National Park in the western part of Africa. Every day he would go out and look for gorillas. Instead of hiding, fighting, or running, he gradually let the gorillas see him. The animals were suspicious at first. They often ran away. But they never hurt Schaller. He was the first to learn that the loud behavior of the male silverback wasn't dangerous. After many patient months he was able to watch several groups of gorillas and record what he found.

One day Schaller was staring at a male gorilla. The gorilla stared back. But when the gorilla was about 20 yards away, he began shaking his head. What did this mean?

Later Schaller stumbled upon a male gorilla and shook his head the way the gorilla had. The gorilla seemed to "read" the shaking head as an act of submission—a sign that Schaller meant no harm. The huge animal wandered away.

Schaller spent about two years in Africa. Later he wrote a book called *The Year of the Gorilla*, which gave the world the first realistic picture of the peaceful, gentle gorilla.

Jane Goodall

In 1957, 23-year-old Jane Goodall boarded an ocean liner called the *Kenya Castle*. She was making her first trip to Africa.

Jane was born in London on April 3, 1934, and grew up in Bournemouth on the southern coast of England. Jane grew up loving animals. She read books like *The Story of Doctor Dolittle* by Hugh Lofting and *The Jungle Book* by Rudyard Kipling. When she was nine, Jane and three of her friends started the Alligator Club. The group went on nature walks and wrote about things they saw. Jane dreamed of one day going to Africa.

One day, after Jane grew up, she got a letter from an old school friend. Her family had moved to a farm in Kenya. Could Jane come for a visit? Jane was thrilled. She worked as a waitress to earn money to buy a round-trip ticket. Four months later, she was on her way.

In Kenya Jane met Louis Leakey, an anthropologist and archaeologist who became famous for his discoveries about Early Man. He had been raised in Africa by his missionary father and knew a great deal about African wildlife. He was working at the Coryndon Museum in Nairobi, Kenya. As luck would have it, his secretary had just quit. Jane jumped at the chance to take her place.

Jane worked with Dr. Leakey for two years. Once she went with Leakey and his wife, Mary, on an expedition to Olduvai Gorge in Tanzania, the site of their archaeological dig. The Leakeys had already found many stone tools used by Early Man. Two years later they would find human bones. Dr. Leakey believed that these bones proved that our earliest human ancestors lived in Africa.

Dr. Leakey was very impressed with how much Jane knew about African animals, even though she did not have a college degree. He talked to her about a group of chimpanzees that lived near Lake Tanganyika. He strongly believed that by studying chimps and how they lived, humans could learn more about how their early ancestors lived. However, studying the chimps might be difficult—and dangerous.

Jane had no training or experience. But she wanted to go and study the chimpanzees more than anything else in the world. At last she told Dr. Leakey how she felt. Dr. Leakey smiled. She was just the person he had wanted to send all along. He knew she had the interest—and the patience—to do a good job.

Jane went back to England. She got a job at a zoo and learned all she could about chimpanzees. Dr. Leakey used his influence to raise money and get permission from the local authorities for the project. A year later, in 1960, Jane began her research at Gombe Stream Reserve in Tanganyika (which is now Tanzania). The authorities, however, did not think it was safe for a 27-year-old woman to go into the jungle alone to study animals. She was told she would have to take someone with her. So Jane took her mother along. After three months her mother went home. But for the next 30 years Jane's life would center on the chimpanzees at Gombe.

Jane lived in a tent and ate out of tin cans. She wore drab clothing so she would not stand out in the forest. It was not easy at first. For a long time she had to study the chimpanzees from a distance, using binoculars.

The chimps gradually became used to Jane. She learned that each chimp has his or her own personality, just as people do. She learned to recognize individual chimps, and she named each one she met. But even then she tried to keep at least 5 yards away. She didn't want her presence to change their behavior.

Throughout the years Jane has "met" more than 300 chimps. She later returned to school and earned a Ph.D. in ethology from Cambridge University. She set up the Gombe Stream Research Center. And in 1975 she founded the Jane Goodall Institute for Wildlife Research, Education and Conservation to promote animal research and conservation efforts throughout the world.

Today Jane spends four months of the year

studying the chimps in Gombe, four writing about her findings, and four traveling around lecturing on her work. Her most recent project is ChimpanZoo, a program that allows students and volunteers at more than fourteen zoos in North America to study chimps in captivity. At the participating zoos the lives of the chimps have already been improved. The chimps live in natural settings instead of small cages. They are fed the sort of food they would eat in the wild.

Almost everything we know about chimpanzees in the wild comes from the work of Jane Goodall. She has fought for humane treatment of chimps in captivity. And she has led worldwide efforts to save the chimp from extinction.

Dian Fossey

Like Jane Goodall, Dian Fossey also grew up with a love for animals. Born in San Francisco in 1932, she had always hoped to be a veterinarian. But at the University of California at Davis, she had trouble with some of her science courses. So she transferred to San Jose State College, graduated with a degree in occupational therapy, and worked with handicapped children at Korsair Children's Hospital in Louisville, Kentucky.

But Dian, like Jane, dreamed about traveling to Africa. In 1963 she went into debt to pay for a trip to Africa and while there met Dr. Leakey at his dig in Olduvai Gorge. Then she went home to work off her debts. Three years later, in March

1966, Dr. Leakey came through Louisville on a lecture tour. At the end of the lecture she pressed her way through the crowd to speak with him. He remembered her and asked her to meet him at eight the next morning.

At their meeting, he told her he needed someone for a long-term field study of the mountain gorillas. He had already turned down twenty-two applicants. He told Dian he wanted her to go—Jane Goodall had proved that women made the best field students. He preferred people who were not trained scientists because they approached their work with "more open minds."

In April 1966, at age 34, Dian went to Central Africa, to the land of the Virunga volcanoes. She set up the Karisoke Research Center on Mount Visoke, the home of the mountain gorilla. And for the rest of her life, it would be her home, too.

At first Dian worked alone with the help of only a few trackers—natives who knew how to track the gorillas through the forest. Every day she went off into the jungle with a stopwatch, a pencil, and paper. When she first made contact with the gorillas, the silverback beat his chest and charged her, trying to scare her away. But Dian developed her own methods of making friends with them. She tape-recorded their sounds and learned to imitate them. She watched their movements, and then she eased her way up to them. She made grunting gorilla sounds. She reached over her head and scratched her neck as if she, too, were an ape. At first the silverback still acted

47

threatened. Then Dian pretended to eat the same leaves the gorillas did. She lowered her eyes and acted submissive.

Gradually, the gorillas began to accept Dian. She began to know them individually and gave them all names. One of her favorites was the old silverback. She named him Digit—which means finger—because his third and fourth fingers were webbed on one hand.

One of the biggest problems for the mountain gorillas was hunters. Sometimes a gorilla was caught and hurt in traps set for other animals. Sometimes poachers came to capture a baby gorilla, who could bring a high price if sold to a zoo. But the only way to capture a baby was to kill its mother and usually several others who tried to protect it. Sometimes the heads and hands of gorillas were cut off to sell as souvenirs.

Dian fought the poachers and spent many hours taking down their traps, ruining their way of earning a living. She made many enemies among native poachers as well as the white Westerners who bought baby gorillas to sell to zoos.

Then one day poachers murdered her beloved Digit and cut off his head and hands. Dian was heartbroken. She began to fight back with all her heart and soul. Because of her reddish-brown hair, some of the natives thought she was a witch. Now Dian played on their belief in witchcraft. She wore Halloween masks and painted "witch signs" on trees with fingernail polish. She tried to scare people into leaving the gorillas alone. Many people praised Dian's strong commitment to save these endangered animals. But most of her assistants did not like the methods she used. Dian would do anything to save what she came to feel were *her* gorillas.

Tragically, on the night of December 28, 1985, she was brutally murdered in her cabin at Karisoke Research Center. The case has yet to be solved. But her work studying the mountain gorilla goes on. Two years before her death, Dian wrote about her work in a book called *Gorillas in the Mist.* Later, a movie by the same name, based on her book, inspired a great deal of interest in her work. And the Digit Fund, which she started, continues to help pay for efforts to save the mountain gorilla.

6

The Future

Once gorillas were thought to be the blood-thirsty enemies of people. Now many scientists fear that the mountain gorilla could become extinct in your lifetime—possibly by the year 2000. People have become the enemy of the great apes —the gorilla, the chimpanzee, the orangutan— and many other animals throughout the world.

For centuries the great apes lived peacefully in the wild. Yet in the twentieth century all the great apes have become *endangered species*. They may no longer be able to survive on their own. And they may become *extinct*—or completely disappear from the Earth.

Poaching continues, even though apes are protected by international law. People cut down forests to make room for villages and farms to feed a growing human population. Trees are chopped down to sell as lumber. People are also destroying acres of rain forests around the world by polluting the atmosphere.

Humans have the ability to adapt. We have the technology to make a home for ourselves almost anywhere on Earth—underwater and even in space. But apes cannot do this. Once their homes are destroyed, they have nowhere to go. And once the great apes vanish from the Earth, we can never bring them back.

What Is Being Done

Many people *do* care about the fate of the great apes. Individuals and organizations around the world work full-time to make sure that endangered animals like the great apes will survive.

Researchers continue to study the great apes in the wild. Their work is often supported by wildlife conservation groups. These groups buy land for animal reserves, create education programs, and work for new international laws to protect endangered species and their natural habitats.

Now there are thousands of national parks and animal reserves throughout the world that ensure good homes for many endangered species. But creating these reserves is not always easy. Do we have the right to march into another nation and tell the people there how to run their country? If the country is poor, it is sometimes hard to stop poachers who earn lots of money for capturing or killing apes. It is hard to explain to a country's leaders why they shouldn't cut down rain forests for farmland when their people are hungry. One idea is to promote animal reserves as tourist attractions. Tourist dollars support the animal reserves *and* contribute to the country's struggling economy.

Today many zoos recognize their role in preserving animals that are disappearing in the wild. Many have replaced small, dirty cages with natural settings. The animals are happier and more likely to have babies, so that zoos no longer need to capture animals in the wild.

There is no one simple answer. Many nations—and many people—must work together to solve the problem of keeping the great apes alive.

What You Can Do

You can make a difference in whether or not the great apes survive. First of all, learn all you can about apes, the environment, and endangered species. Hundreds of species of animals become extinct each year. But many nonprofit organizations are working hard to make sure that the great apes will continue to exist.

The National Geographic Society, the African Wildlife Foundation, the World Wildlife Foundation, and many other groups are trying to save endangered species from extinction.

Jane Goodall is working to save chimpanzees in the wild and to improve conditions for chimps in zoos and labs. To find out more about her work, write: Jane Goodall Institute for Wildlife Research, Education and Conservation, P.O. Box 26846, Tucson, Arizona 85726.

Want to learn more about Penny Patterson's work? Want to join Koko's fan club? Write to the Gorilla Foundation, Box 620-530, Woodside, California 94062.

If you'd like to be an official "Friend of Washoe," write to Friends of Washoe, Central Washington University, Ellensburg, Washington 98926.

What else can you do? Share what you learn with your friends and family and teachers so that they'll become involved, too.

The great apes are in great danger—but it's not too late to save them. You can help make sure that these fascinating animals are around for the next generation to study and enjoy.